HOW TO BE
A PREGNANT
FATHER

HOW TO BE A PREGNANT FATHER

**An illustrated survival guide for the first-time father
by Peter Mayle   illustrated by Arthur Robins**

Including the Pregnant Father's Cookbook by Len Deighton.

PAN BOOKS LTD
LONDON, SYDNEY AND AUCKLAND

For Murray and Gail, but mostly for Murray.

(Also respectfully dedicated to the male sea-horse, who not only carries the eggs but delivers the babies.)

First published 1977 by Lyle Stuart Inc.

This edition published 1993 by Pan Books Ltd
a division of Pan Macmillan Publishers Limited
Cavaye Place London SW10 9PG
and Basingstoke

Associated companies throughout the world

ISBN 0-330-33111-6

Copyright © Peter Mayle 1977

The right of Peter Mayle to be identified as the
author of this work has been asserted by him in accordance
with the Copyright, Designs and Patents Act 1988.

9 8 7 6 5 4 3 2 1

A CIP catalogue record for this book is available from
the British Library

Printed in Hong Kong

CONGRATULATIONS!

UNLESS you're reading this book under false pretences, you have just become a pregnant father. Traditionally, this is a time in a man's life when he becomes a rather uneasy background figure, hovering on the fringes of the great event. From time to time, catalogues of baby's clothing and equipment may be thrust under his nose; or his opinion may occasionally be sought on the size and design of the crib or the baby carriage.

But in between helping to conceive the child and giving out cigars at the other end of the process, very little attention has been paid to the man's side of pregnancy.

And, most definitely, there *is* a man's side.

For the first-time father, pregnancy can be puzzling, tiring and sometimes hurtful, and a frequent strain on the patience and the digestion.

The most unsettling fact to face is that your dear, familiar wife will change. She will change not only in shape, but also in disposition. She will be subject to uncharacteristic moods and fancies, often following one another with confusing speed.

She smiles, she weeps, she feels ravenous or

bilious, she wants company, she wants solitude – all in the course of the same day and quite possibly even before lunchtime.

You, sir, have months of this to cope with.

Whether you have a good pregnancy or a miserable one depends largely on your attitude. If you're prepared to become a player in this nine-month event rather than just a spectator, you'll enjoy it. Furthermore, you'll make things a lot easier for your wife.

This book is based on the assumption that you actually want to join in. And the best time to do that is at the very beginning.

The most crucial period in setting the mood of your pregnancy is now; your behaviour during these first few pregnant weeks is vital. This, unfortunately, is a problem. Because once the initial excitement has died down, the chances are that you'll start to worry.

Can we afford it? Do we need somewhere bigger to live? Supposing it's twins? What happens to the holiday we've planned? Will we have to get rid of the sports car? Will we have to get rid of our sex life? Complications! Hospitals! Doctor's bills! Midnight feedings! No more lazy Sunday mornings! No more freedom! No more parties! Panic! Help!

Calm down. These are the worries that beset almost every pregnant father, and you will find that they can be resolved quite comfortably over the next nine months.

In the meantime, your wife needs all the attention you can give her. She, after all, is trying to get used to the idea of carrying a small human being around inside her, which is an infinitely more unsettling experience than anything you think you're going through.

So in these early stages, keep your neuroses to yourself. If you start worrying out loud, your wife's going to think you don't want the baby. And if she ever starts thinking that, you're both going to have a bad pregnancy.

Of course, your wife may bring some of these things up herself. If she does, by all means talk them over with her. But if all she wants to do for the first couple of weeks of pregnancy is talk about

the joys of parenthood, don't spoil it for her. You have nine months to sort out the practical details. A few days dreaming about your genius offspring will do you both good.

While you're still in that happy state of pre-parental euphoria, here are one or two simple and constructive things you can do to start your pregnancy off on the right foot.

Celebrate

There will be plenty of time for eating and drinking sensibly in the months ahead. But for one glorious evening, as early on in the pregnancy as possible, take your wife out for an extravagant dinner. Buy her flowers, take taxis, have all the forbidden delights on the menu, have liqueurs, have fun. Eat, drink and be merry, for tomorrow you diet. But on this self-indulgent night, enjoy the fact that you're *both* having a baby.

Learn about the inner woman

You'll find it useful and fascinating to find out exactly what is going on inside your wife's body.

There are literally hundreds of books that describe in loving detail almost every minute of a woman's pregnancy. Your wife will probably have

at least one of these books herself. Read it. Find out what happens to the mother month by month as the bump grows into a baby.

You'll discover that it's quite normal for a pregnant woman to have cramps and cravings, to feel occasional nausea and irritability. It's not an unkind fate that has singled her out for special attention; it's life.

In this case, a little knowledge is a helpful thing. It is far easier to be sympathetic to your wife when you know what she's going through.

But the main reason you should be on speaking terms with the mysteries of pregnancy is that it will make the whole business more interesting for you, the pregnant father. And let us not forget that the purpose of this book is to make *your* pregnancy a happy one.

Make every pregnant month count

Pregnancy provides you with a splendid opportunity to catch up on all kinds of things you've been meaning to do for ages.

As the months go by, your social life will probably become progressively quieter. Unborn babies are not fond of late nights and parties. They find too much food or drink disagreeable, and if forced to endure a heavy evening, they take their revenge the following morning by making their mother feel dreadful.

So you will find yourselves with more free evenings than you've had for some time.

This is the moment to read The Gulag Archipelago, instead of pretending you have. Or to take up backgammon, as everyone else seems to have done with such smug proficiency. In fact, it

doesn't really matter what you turn your hand to – cooking, Kung Fu, model making, racehorse handicapping, dirty Scrabble – as long as you take up something that makes use of that time.

Pregnant fathers fall into two distinct categories: those who use the pregnancy as an excuse for idleness, and those who use it to accomplish something – even if it's only reading some long-neglected books.

Invariably, those who used the pregnancy constructively had more fun and happier wives than those who vegetated.

Don't neglect the outer woman

If you value your wife's well-being during this time, never forget that her basic feelings have not changed simply because her shape has. On the contrary, she is probably more sensitive now than ever before, particularly about your feelings towards her.

Do you love her? Do you find her attractive?

Then let her know. Give her flowers, buy her perfume, notice her hair – treat her, in other words, like the woman she is. Not like some strange creature who has ceased to be feminine until she has hatched her egg.

Naturally, you would never make such an elementary mistake. Or would you? Does she really feel happy and loved?

If you're not sure, give her a kiss and one last glass of champagne before reading the next chapter.

Don't just sit there, do something

Your wife's body, which has hitherto been the exclusive property of your wife, is now being shared by a passenger.

And one of the least pleasant side-effects of this often starts very early on in the pregnancy, long before any bumps or bulges appear. It is, of course, that special kind of awful feeling known as morning sickness.

Unfortunately, as men have never experienced morning sickness, many of them are tempted to dismiss it as a display of feminine dramatics, designed to attract sympathy and attention. They couldn't be more wrong.

Morning sickness is a very real and inconvenient problem. Furthermore, it makes those women who suffer from it feel not only ill, but frequently depressed as well. Whatever you do, don't under-estimate it.

An example of how it actually feels comes from a woman whose hobbies are having babies and sailing small boats. She has had considerable experience of both morning sickness and seasickness, and she claims the two feelings are quite similar.

So if you'd like some idea of what your wife is going through, go sailing and get seasick one weekend. You may feel a lot more sympathetic towards her condition once you've had a taste of something like it yourself.

Don't let all this get you down. Normally, morning sickness only lasts for two or three months. And there is an even chance that your wife will go through the entire pregnancy without a single queasy moment.

As you might expect in these computerized times, there is in existence a set of statistics telling us how many pregnant women suffer from morning sickness, and how many don't.

According to this particular set of figures, 50 per cent of mothers *did* find themselves diving uncontrollably for the nearest bathroom during pregnancy; the other half had no trouble at all.

Let's hope your wife is one of the fortunate 50 per cent. If she's not (and you'll know within the first couple of months), you must be prepared to take some rather unusual precautions.

In really severe cases, the only sensible thing to do is go and see your doctor. But if it's just normally awful, you may find the following hints are of some help.

They're split into three sections that cover **home sickness, travelling sickness and away** sickness at various times. (Because despite its name, morning sickness is not necessarily confined to the morning.)

At home

It's normal for morning sickness, like charity, to begin at home. And what often sets it off is the sight and smell of fried eggs, sausages and bacon.

If you feel unable to face the world without a fried breakfast, you would be wise to learn to cook it yourself, and be prepared to eat alone. Even the bravest pregnant stomach may find that kind of onslaught difficult to take first thing in the morning.

A much more sympathetic alternative is to change your breakfast menu. Try, for instance, grapefruit, toast and a boiled egg.

Something like that is easy to prepare, less offensive to the pregnant disposition, and much better for you than all that fried stuff anyway.

The kitchen is not the only place where you might have to change your early morning habits. As you can imagine, many battles in the war against morning sickness are fought in the bathroom.

Here, the great thing is to be in readiness at all times for instant retreat.

If you're having a leisurely shave, and there's a frantic hammering on the door, it's no use asking your wife to wait until you've finished.

She can't. The consequences of keeping her waiting are too ghastly to discuss.

So be on your toes, and when the moment comes take prompt evasive action.

One last thought before we leave the bathroom.

Unless your wife specifically asks you to stay with her, make yourself scarce while she is coming to terms with her stomach. Being sick is a messy and unattractive business, and most women prefer to do it in private.

Travelling

There's no need to stay rooted at home throughout your pregnancy.

But it's wrong to assume that you can travel about freely as soon as the morning is over. Morning sickness has been known to happen in a late afternoon traffic jam or a crowded city street, with spectacular results. You just can't be too careful.

Preferably, you should avoid public transport.

Much as they might want to help, bus and train drivers can't make unscheduled stops to accommodate the demands of an uneasy stomach.

And taxi drivers, faced with the prospect of a passenger about to throw up, are likely to be more concerned with their upholstery than your wife's discomfort.

But what if, like most of us, she *has* to use public transport?

She probably won't be allowed to take travel sickness pills. She can't predict when she's going to feel ill. She can't ask the driver to stop.

No, there's only one answer. It may not be elegant, but it does provide a small measure of comfort, and it can be taken *everywhere* (even to the movies).

It is the regulation airline sick-bag, complete with sealable top.

This won't stop your wife from feeling sick, or indeed from being sick. But it does mean that she has something to be sick in. Also, she can remove all traces of the catastrophe for discreet disposal later on.

Pregnant women who have tried this simple device have found it surprisingly comforting, and say that it does help to reduce the panic that often accompanies sickness in a public place.

As for the receptacle itself, the airline bags are best. Airlines, after all, had them well made, and we have never heard of one failing yet. Ask your travelling friends to bring some back for you whenever they fly, or write to the Public Relations Officer of an airline, and ask him for a supply.

Of course, if you're lucky enough never to have to use public transport, the problem is lessened considerably. You can usually pull in to the side of the road.

Nevertheless, we still recommend a supply of airline bags in the glove box, just in case.

Without going into details of the unpleasant episode during the late afternoon traffic jam, suffice it to say that one airline bag, accurately used, would have saved a great deal of embarrassment all round.

In other people's homes

When you, your wife and her delicate disposition go visiting, all three of you will have a better time if you prepare the ground first.

This is definitely a job for you, rather than your wife. She probably dislikes making a fuss, and would prefer to keep quiet and hope for the best.

Courageous though this is, it is courting disaster.

Consider, for example, a small dinner party at a friend's house. Supposing your wife is served something that makes her feel ill on sight? Supposing she's been seated in a corner, where she has to clamber over two other guests and a potted plant to get away from the table? Supposing she's not sure *exactly* where the bathroom is?

The possibilities are enough to make you lose your appetite completely. However, these horrors can be avoided with the help of a few words from you.

Presumably, your friends will know that your wife's expecting a baby. You should warn them *well in advance* that she's also expecting to feel ill from time to time.

With luck, they will then ask you if there's any kind of food your wife can't face eating. If they don't ask, tell them. Otherwise you might be one guest short for the evening.

(A seemingly harmless bowl of spaghetti once caused a pregnant guest to barricade herself in the bathroom for two and a half hours. The other guests, with embarrassing courtesy, delayed starting their meal until the lady emerged. The evening was not a success.)

Seating is almost as important as eating. Ideally, your wife should be placed as far away from kitchen smells as possible, with a clear avenue of escape to the bathroom. If there's some fresh air around, she should be near that too.

Finally, both of you should know the way to the bathroom before you sit down. And find out about any small peculiarities it may have, such as cunningly concealed lavatories or obscurely placed light switches. The middle of a crisis is no time to be fumbling around in the dark.

Having done your homework, you can relax. You've done all you can. From now on, you're in the lap of the gods.

CRAVINGS:
in which we discover that an insane desire for a peanut butter, pickle and chocolate sandwich on date nut bread is absolutely nothing to be alarmed about.

Having tiptoed through the delicate ordeal of morning sickness, you may be tempted to breathe a sigh of relief and look forward to a return to normality at meal times.

Don't sigh too soon.

It's quite possible that your wife's appetite will undergo a complete change. Instead of feeling faint at the sight of a boiled egg, she may begin to consume, with great relish, a curious mixture of foods that would make a strong man recoil.

This doesn't happen to all pregnant women. Your wife could go through the entire pregnancy with nothing more exotic than a lamb chop passing her lips. However, you should be prepared for the alternative – a desperate, almost addictive desire for some truly extraordinary flavour combinations.

These gastronomic adventures are called cravings. Why should they happen to some women and not to others? Why should they happen at all? Medical science offers no precise answers, so we'll try to provide our own.

It seems reasonable to assume that cravings occur as a result of the changes taking place in one of these two broad areas.

1. Physical

There are cases where a woman's everyday diet is not sufficiently balanced to meet the nutritional demands of pregnancy. She and the unborn baby may not be getting enough of certain vitamins, minerals or protein. So the body adjusts, and translates the need for the missing fuel into an appetite for foods that will correct the deficiency.

This is rare. In an age of multi-vitamin tablets, balanced diets and excellent medical supervision, it is far more likely that the cause will be

2. Emotional

Cravings are so varied and unpredictable that it's impossible to forecast the form they will take. One women's peanuts and pineapple chunks may be another woman's tuna fish and cheesecake.

Putting aside the ingredients for a moment, and assuming that the craving is not based on physical need, what is it that makes a normal woman with normal appetites suddenly go bananas in the kitchen?

The answer is that, consciously or subconsciously, she's trying to tell you something. It may be any, or all, of the following.

"I'm worried"

Having a baby, particularly the first one, can be a disturbing experience. Physical and emotional changes are taking place in your wife; and since you're not going through them yourself, it's difficult for you to share them. Sympathetic as you may be, you're in the position of a spectator, and she has to cope with these changes pretty much alone.

Frequently, this will make her anxious. You'd be anxious, too, if you were in her shoes. As you know, one of the most common reactions to anxiety is to head for the welcoming shelves of the fridge and take comfort in food.

"I'm not attractive"

As your wife changes in shape, she might well feel less and less sexually attractive. Gone, for the moment, is the sylph-like figure. As the months stretch ahead of her, so does an ever-expanding stomach and, she thinks, the possibility of a less attentive husband.

If she has the slightest reason to believe these misgivings, she might come to the conclusion that if she's not going to be sexy, she might as well be full. Bring on the ice cream, the sweets, the chocolate cake and the desserts. Bring on the pasta and potatoes and bread. Let joy and the waistline be unconfined.

This, of course, will probably produce exactly the effect she was worried about in the first place. But it happens.

"I'm not loved"

One of the easiest signals of all to spot, because it often occurs at dead of night.

It is two o'clock in the morning, when an insistent hand shakes you awake. Is it burglars? Is it labour pains? Is the house on fire?

No, it is not. It's a request for fresh raspberries (which are invariably out of season), or a hot roast beef sandwich with a dozen baked oysters, or something else equally complicated. And you will have no rest until the order is filled.

Basically, all these cravings are not for food. They're for *attention*. If you can satisfy that particular hunger, the eating orgies won't be necessary.

There is no formula in existence that you can invoke to reassure your wife that you *do* love her, you *do* find her attractive, you *do* want the baby, and that millions of other women have gone through childbirth and lived to tell the tale. It's a very personal area, and you, better than any book, should know how best to treat your wife.

But as you've never been in this situation before, perhaps we can offer a few practical suggestions which may help to combat the cravings.

Are you more comforting than a litre of ice cream?

When cravings strike, your wife can either head for the calories or for you. It's a straight contest - you versus the fridge, and the winner is the one who offers the most solace.

Perhaps you think we're making a problem out of a few simple snacks. After all, the woman's pregnant. Why shouldn't she indulge herself? What harm can a few extra pounds do?

Quite a lot, as your doctor will tell you.

Perhaps the most common complication in otherwise straightforward pregnancies is excessive weight gain and obesity caused by over-eating. It can lead to prolonged labour. Caesarean section, premature birth, or toxemia. A less serious, but unsightly, result of carrying around too much weight can be varicose veins. And if you're still not convinced, you should know that every excess pound put on during pregnancy is more than normally difficult to diet off after the birth.

Your wife's doctor will almost certainly give her a diet designed to give her and the baby the necessary nutrition without excess weight gain. Take a look at the diet, take an interest in it, and do all you can to see that your wife sticks to it. You're not doing her or the baby any favours if you encourage cheating.

Fortunately, given the choice between a slab of chocolate cake and some affection and understanding from you, your wife will probably choose you. But be prepared. This will involve a good deal more than a half-hearted hug and some vague words of encouragement. Here are some ways you can help.

A shared diet is an easier diet

Your wife would need the self-control of a saint to be content with a salad while she watches you put away a steak and hot chips followed by a chocolate sundae.

The least you can do is meet her half way at mealtimes. We're not suggesting you starve yourself; but why not try to follow her diet for one meal a day? Dinner is best, obviously, as that's the meal you're most often together, and the time when her resistance to forbidden foods is at its lowest.

This idea has three distinct advantages.

First, your wife will appreciate the constructive effort you're making to help her. And it *will* help; she'll find it much easier to stick to doctor's orders if she can see that you take them seriously too.

Second, you'll both try to find ways of making the diet interesting if you're both eating it. Anything, from a lettuce leaf to a pot roast, can be either bland or tasty depending on its preparation. As your wife won't be cooking two separate dinners, she can concentrate on making the diet delicious.

Third, you yourself will probably lose a few pounds. And we don't know of anyone who wouldn't look better for losing a few pounds. Including you.

Put the larder on a diet

If, like Oscar Wilde, you can resist everything except temptation, the smartest thing you can do is to put the temptation firmly out of reach.

Go through the contents of your fridge, preferably in the morning when you won't be so tempted to cheat, and take out all the things you've both agreed not to eat. Give them *immediately* to the kids next door, before you have a chance to weaken. And don't replace them on your next trip to the supermarket.

Saying goodbye to doughnuts and ice cream may be a wrench, but it's not for ever. And you can console yourself with the thought that this small act of abstinence is good for both of you.

If either of you is a snack addict, you may find it impossible not to have something to nibble on from time to time. Try fresh fruit instead of biscuits, yoghurt and honey instead of desserts, cheese instead of sweets. These alternatives don't provide the same guilty satisfaction as junk food, but they are better than nothing, and a lot better for you. And who knows – they may develop into a healthy habit.

Keep your lunches to yourself

Five times a week, you'll have the opportunity to eat what you want without causing your wife a single pang of jealousy. Unless you work at home, your lunches from Monday to Friday are private matters between you and your digestion.

For heaven's sake, keep them that way. Don't go into rhapsodies over the duck à l'orange; don't bring home the chef's recipe for chocolate soufflé; don't even complain about the steak and kidney pie in the pub being a little heavy. Otherwise you may end up wearing your dinner instead of eating it.

And who could blame your wife for getting mad? She's on a diet 24 hours a day, and a mouthful-by-mouthful account of your adventures through the menu isn't going to help her keep to it.

So, for the next few months, save the food talk until you can both go out and enjoy a

five-course meal. Exceeding the feed limit, if you have to do it at all, is not something to brag about.

P.S. The truth about "eating for two"

It's a fallacy. A normally healthy woman needs very little extra food during pregnancy – between 5% and 10% more calories than usual, and about 5% more protein. Women who use pregnancy as an excuse to eat twice as much as normal are asking for trouble, both during labor and during the slimming down period afterwards.

SEX:
what to do about it and when to do without it.

In the opening weeks of pregnancy, the first-time father traditionally behaves as though his wife has suddenly been transformed from flesh and blood into a delicate piece of china. Doors are opened, packages carried, cushions are provided and a robust young woman is treated like an ailing octogenarian.

All this attention is fine; your wife will enjoy it and it will do her good. But one place she won't want to be treated like an untouchable relic is in the bedroom.

Whatever you may have heard, unless you have specific medical orders to the contrary, sex during pregnancy can and should go on for as long as you both feel like it – certainly up to the eighth month and sometimes beyond. Obviously, there are adjustments to make, which we'll come to later. The main thing to remember, though, is that a healthy sex urge doesn't disappear just because a baby is on the way. Yours hasn't, and neither has your wife's.

Often, quite the reverse happens. Freed from the worries of an unwanted pregnancy, and able to throw caution and contraceptives to the wind, the pregnant woman can relax completely and enjoy lovemaking more fully and more frequently than before. In fact, there will probably be times when your wife will be more interested in having sex than you.

Even so, you may find that there is a pendulum pattern to her desire for sex. Because of the changes taking place in her emotions and her hormones, the extremes of desire or lack of it can be more pronounced than either of you have been used to. There's nothing she can do about it, so don't get upset if she occasionally doesn't feel like making love when you do. Be patient. Pendulums always swing back.

One of the most basic requirements for a relaxed sex life during pregnancy is an understanding of what's going on inside your wife's body. When you know what's happening, it's easier to make the necessary sexual adjustments. So right at the start, we strongly recommend that *both* of you should go to the doctor.

If there are any potential problems (such as a history of miscarriages in either of your families), both of you should hear about them straight from the doctor's mouth. If there's nothing to worry about, both of you should hear that too. A joint visit reduces the chances of misunderstanding between you and your wife. It's a nice way to demonstrate to her that you really do intend to share the pregnancy. And you'll find it not only reassuring, but fascinating.

If you haven't made an appointment yet, do it now. Meanwhile, here are a few general aspects of sex during pregnancy to think about while you're in the waiting room.

Some sexual days off

Although you can look forward to an active sex life for most of the pregnancy, there are certain times during the nine months when you should take it easy or abstain altogether.

It comes as a surprise to most men to learn that the time to exercise the greatest sexual caution is not just at the end of the pregnancy, but at the beginning too. Your wife, for the first

few weeks, may show no outward signs of her condition other than a slightly more voluptuous mid-section. Don't let this lead you into thinking that nothing much is going on. The most fundamental part of pregnancy – when the fertilized egg is developing into a tiny human being – takes place during the first three months. And with babies, as with many other forms of life, the first weeks of growth are the most vulnerable. That's why the vast majority of miscarriages happen within three months of conception.

This is not to say you should move your bed out into the living room. But if you've been in the habit of enjoying a particularly acrobatic sex life, now's the time to calm it down a little. There are certain days when it's wise to forget about sex completely – the days when your wife would normally be having a period, and the twelfth week. Check with your doctor.

He or she may also suggest a sexual postponement during the last two months, but that depends more on individual cases.

Apart from medically prescribed days off, there's nothing to stop you from making love whenever you both want to. But even when the spirit is willing, the flesh may be weak enough to cause you to make some changes in your normal routine.

Night time's not always the right time

The chances are that you, like most of us, are limited in your opportunities for lovemaking by the demands made on your time by work. With your days spent in the office, sex has to be fitted in first thing in the morning or at night. During pregnancy, even these few hours are in jeopardy due to circumstances beyond your control.

For instance, let's take a typical weekday early morning. There you are, half-awake and full of affectionate lust. Gently, you start to nuzzle your wife into consciousness. She wakes. She groans. She heads hurriedly for the bathroom. By the time she has recovered sufficiently from her bout of morning sickness to think about sex, you're dictating your first letter in the office.

Undaunted, you determine to try again that night. You get home, and have an early dinner. You yawn, pointedly. She yawns. Off you go to bed, full of wicked intentions.

Alas, her yawn wasn't a hint; it was genuine. She's exhausted from carrying around her embryonic passenger, and falls into a deep sleep while you're brushing your teeth.

What's to be done? With the best will in the world, you can't fight morning sickness. And the further you get into the pregnancy, the more tired your wife is going to be by bedtime.

There is a solution, however, which has worked wonders for several pregnant couples we know. It's a delightful institution called the naked cocktail hour.

Here's how it works. You forget the usual sequence of a couple of drinks, followed by dinner, followed by bed. Instead, you make for the bedroom as soon as you get home. Your wife will be less tired, and more likely to feel like making love. It will give you a sharpened appetite for dinner. And it's a lot more fun than a

dry martini. Try it and see.

Finally, make the most of weekends to catch up on your lovemaking. For two days a week, the clock doesn't matter. If you feel like going to bed in the early afternoon and having breakfast at midnight, do it. Try to keep your weekends free from social obligations. Your sex life is far more important than a game of golf or a dinner date.

Positions

As the months go by, your wife is going to find it either uncomfortable or impossible to make love with the unrestrained enthusiasm of pre-pregnant days. Certain positions are out as the bulk of the baby comes between you – notably the classic missionary style. This can even be dangerous, as can any position which involves deep penetration by the penis.

Luckily, there are still plenty of safe and satisfying variations to choose from. Without attempting to catalogue them, here's one well-tried favourite that you can enjoy well into the final weeks.

It is the safest, and probably the best, position for pregnant lovemaking: both of you lie on your side, facing the same direction, so that you enter the vagina from behind. This gives you full use of one hand, limited use of the other, and makes dangerously deep penetration impossible. And obviously, since the baby is on the other side of the activity, the position will work no matter how big the bulge becomes.

You'll find your own variations as you experiment, but keep away from anything violently athletic in favour of gentler techniques with shallower penetration. Make full use of your fingers and tongue. Try mutual masturbation. With ingenuity and practice, you'll discover a few sexual extras that will still be giving you pleasure when your baby's gone to college.

Keep on hugging

Despite all your mutual willingness and ingenuity, the day will come when you will have to call a temporary halt to full sexual activity. Unless you have hyperactive sex drives, this shouldn't bother you. In fact, there seems to be a natural sexual lull at the end of most pregnancies when both of you are quite happy to give it a rest.

But be warned. Many men make the mistake of linking sex with affection. As one stops, so does the other.

This couldn't happen at a worse time, as far as your wife is concerned. If she is like most women, the last stage of pregnancy will be an apprehensive and physically uncomfortable few weeks. She needs reassurance and she needs affection, which you can no longer express through lovemaking. If there is ever a time to be more affectionate, more attentive and more loving than usual, this is it. Over to you.

IS THIS THE REAL THING?
Is it indigestion?
How do you know when it's time to go?

The neat and tidy theoretical pregnancy lasts for 280 days, or 10 lunar months of 28 days each. Real life is less predictable. Based on the information you have supplied, your doctor will give you an approximate birth date – and probably a warning not to take it too literally. Babies, being only human, are seldom that punctual, and first babies in particular have a tendency not to arrive on schedule. So don't put too much trust in the calendar. You'll be much better off if you learn to recognize the signals that babies send out to let you know they're on their way out.

To be able to spot the true symptoms (as opposed to the false alarms, which we come to later), it helps to know a little about the baby's travels from womb to delivery room.

The final stretch

By the end of the ninth month, your baby is about 18 inches long and weighs several pounds. To get out into the world, he or she has to pass through the mouth of the womb, normally a tiny opening and only about four inches across when it's fully expanded. From there, progress continues down the vagina and out in the open. The process demands miraculous elasticity, and involves a lot of hard work on the part of both mother and child. Whoever called it labour wasn't kidding.

Labour is divided into three distinct stages. We've given indications of how long each stage takes, but they are only indications, and can vary enormously. As a general rule, though, first babies take longer to make the trip than any brothers or sisters who may arrive in years to come.

Stage One

Often called the Dilation Period, because this is the stage during which the mouth of the womb is stretched until there is space for the baby to pass through. The stretching is caused by the muscles of the womb. They contract, pushing the baby down towards its eventual exit.

True labour contractions can be recognized by their regular pattern: at first, they're fairly far apart, perhaps every 15 minutes. And they don't last very long – only about 10 seconds. As labour continues, these contractions happen more often, last longer and are more intense.

Once they start, remember to time them before you call the doctor, otherwise it's difficult to tell how far things have gone.

Another sign that the baby's intentions about leaving the womb are serious is the 'show', a discharge of blood and mucus from the vagina. This can often happen without your noticing, especially at night, so don't count on spotting it. In any case, the frequency of the contractions will tell you all you need to know, show or no show.

This first stage of labour is by far the longest. At the risk of depressing both of you, it can last for 24 hours or more. On the other hand, it can be all over in 90 minutes. Both are quite normal. Mercifully, the long-lasting labours are usually less painful, as the contractions tend to be shorter and less intense.

Stage Two

The beginning of what is called the Expulsion Period is usually marked by an event described in rather spectacular terms as 'the breaking of the waters'. Sounds like the title of an epic movie, but all it means is that the sac full of fluid that has protected the baby for nine months has broken. Pressure from the contractions which have been pushing the baby towards the mouth of the womb causes a rupture in the sac. The fluid then escapes – in a gush or a trickle. Either way, it is normally a sign that the baby is making its way down the birth canal. (Not always the case, however. The waters can break much earlier. Again, the only foolproof guide to what's happening is the frequency of the contractions.)

The baby's progress down the birth canal, which ends in the actual delivery, takes anything from 30 minutes to an hour and a half under normal conditions. But even though the baby has appeared, more is yet to come.

Stage Three

The birth of the baby is followed shortly afterwards by the expulsion of the afterbirth. This is about the size of a soup plate, and it is the tissue through which the baby has been getting its rations of food and oxygen from the mother. Baby and food supply were joined together by the umbilical cord, which by now will have been snipped off.

Time for this last stage: about 15 minutes.

That, very briefly, is the normal sequence of events. Since most of the action will take place under medical supervision, there's no need to concern yourself with the fine points of delivery technique. What you should know, however, is when it's time to go. Too soon, and your wife has to hang around in the hospital, which isn't as pleasant for her as hanging around at home with you. Too late, and you might find yourself wishing you'd watched Dr. Kildare more closely.

To complicate matters, there are the false alarms we mentioned earlier. Many a doctor has been routed out of bed at 3 a.m. only to find that what you thought were contractions were wind pains in disguise.

So for your own peace of mind, and to preserve good relations with your doctor, you should be able to tell the difference between the false alarm and the genuine article.

False alarms

Stomach cramps, a few unexpected kicks from the baby and plain old indigestion have all caused their share of premature panic. So have 'dropping pains', which are caused by the lowering of the womb inside the body some four weeks before the birth.

While these symptoms may not indicate the start of the main event, don't dismiss them as minor irritations. They are invariably uncomfortable, and often painful. The most effective general remedy we've come across for these assorted aches is for your wife to kneel on all fours. Most women find this brings partial or total relief; it's also a good position to try when true labour starts.

As for distinguishing between true and false labour, all you need is your watch. If the symptoms come at odd intervals without any pattern, they may be uncomfortable but they're not labour pains. Be guided by timing; in fact, it's best to write down when the pains occur. If you rely on a flustered memory it's easy to make mistakes.

The real thing

Just when you've resigned yourself to sitting out the world's first fifteen-month pregnancy, something stirs. It's your wife, more restless than usual and complaining of a feeling of pressure in the small of her back.

This is it. The pressure is caused by the growing tension in the muscles of the womb, and is the prelude to the rhythmical contractions which will now gradually develop.

Time them carefully – how often they come and how long they last. When they come *regularly*

every ten minutes or so, call your doctor. (It's not worth calling before unless the waters have broken or the 'show' has appeared; if either happens, call at once.)

The best thing to do when your wife's in labour

Your contribution during labour can make all the difference to the birth, and your wife's feelings about it afterwards. Whether she remembers it as a shared experience or a solitary ordeal is up to you.

As a general rule, the more you can be with her during the various stages, the better – including the actual birth, providing that's what you both want and hospital regulations permit.

Some women prefer to give birth without the father being present. Some men have been known to faint in the delivery room. And maybe because of that, many hospitals don't allow the father in until it's time for him to meet his baby. So if you want to be at the birth, make arrangements well in advance with your doctor and the hospital.

Let's assume you want to be there and you want to be helpful. What can you *do*? After all, the place is full of experts who deliver more babies in a week than you'll see in a lifetime.

Leave them to take care of the business arrangements; you concentrate on comfort and encouragement.

Be there to rub your wife's back when contractions come. Be there to hold her hand when it hurts. Be there to cool her forehead, to talk to her, to tell her you love her.

But above all, be there. It's the best pain reliever there is.

YOUR HOSPITAL SURVIVAL KIT,
and a guide to who's who in the waiting room.

You've called the doctor. You've called the hospital. With monumental aplomb, you are about to step out of the front door immaculately clad in checked sports coat and striped pyjama bottoms.

You think this kind of thing only happens in films? It happens to real people too. However well prepared you think you are for the hospital trip, when it's time to go your first instinct is to rush headlong for the maternity ward.

Relax. Let your wife be an example to you. For some mysterious and wonderful reason best known to nature, the pregnant woman whose time has come is almost always serene, unworried and totally in command of her situation. She is, of course, confident that you have taken care of your side of the arrangements. You have?

Excellent. Then you won't be worried by questions like these:

Do you know the way?

You have probably only been to the hospital once before, when you made the initial reservation. In the subsequent months, construction work on the road and a new one-way traffic system could add 25 nerve-wracking minutes to the trip. Worse still, they could cause you to get lost. There's also a 50/50 chance that you'll have to make the drive at night, when unfamiliar roads look even more unfamiliar. Have we given you enough reasons to make a dry run to the hospital one night soon – before you have to do it for real?

Is your car ready for fatherhood?

If there's one occasion during the year when your car will have an attack of temperament, you can bet that this will be it.

Keep the tank full of petrol. Check the tyres regularly. Check the battery. And as a failsafe, find a sympathetic neighbour who will lend you his car if catastrophe strikes yours.

Quick! Where's a taxi?

A taxi is a great way to avoid all the possible horrors we've just outlined – always providing you can find one when you need it. In times of emergency, as in times of rain and snow, cabs tend to vanish. For safety's sake, arm yourself with the telephone numbers of not one, but two, 24-hour radio cab companies. And when you call, don't take slow for an answer. Explain the circumstances, and you'll get quicker service than you'd ever believed possible.

Cab-drivers are fathers too.

Assuming you have the business of getting to the hospital well in hand, we can now concentrate on what you'll be taking there.

For some weeks now, you have probably been aware of a curious ritual taking place at odd

intervals in the bedroom. It consists of your wife, a suitcase and an ever-changing selection of contents. The smaller the suitcase, the more often it gets unpacked and re-packed. In its quieter moments, it stands at the ready by the bedroom door.

The basic contents are items suggested by most hospitals in a kind effort to be helpful – the things they feel your wife will need during her first couple of days as a new mother. If only they knew what complications are triggered off by the sight of a simple list.

The list is, of course, more than adequate for two or three days. The trouble is that most first-time mothers feel a compulsion to pack for a week or more. And how many women can put everything they think they *may* need for an entire week into one small case ? Without even considering the baby's wardrobe, there are nightgowns, robes, street clothes, hair dryers, cosmetics, books, magazines and heaven knows what else to cram in. Hence the ritual in the bedroom and, often, the sly substitution of larger and larger suitcases. We have seen couples panting up to the maternity desk with enough equipment to mount an attempt on Everest. A few days in the hospital? They bring enough to withstand a six-month siege.

If you can find some way to avoid taking a cabin trunk to hospital, your departure from home will be quicker, easier and less likely to give you a hernia. We suggest you pick your moment and make a deal with your wife. She agrees to take the absolute minimum suggested by the hospital in *one small bag*. In return, you agree to provide a shuttle service between home and hospital, delivering what she needs on your daily visits.

One important advantage of this system is that it leaves you with a free hand to carry your own emergency supplies. And you're certainly going to need something to sustain you through those hours in the waiting room. Maternity hospitals are superbly designed for maternity, but the facilities for pregnant fathers are usually modest : a handful of dog-eared magazines, a few hard chairs and coffee with a distinct whiff of disinfectant is about all you can expect.

The survival kit which we now recommend has been tested in the field. It can be prepared well in advance, carried in one hand, and should provide a measure of comfort and diversion during your vigil.

A standard airline shoulder-bag will be quite large enough for :

- A small transistor radio. Most models come equipped with an earplug attachment, so you can listen without disturbing anyone else.

- A long but uncomplicated book. Your powers of concentration will be limited, so don't pack anything too intellectually demanding.

- The address and opening hours of the nearest take-away food shop. As long as you avoid peak times you should be able to pick up something hot to eat and be back in position quite quickly.

- A large bag full of 10p pieces.

- Names and phone numbers of all the people you want to call the minute your first-born makes an appearance. (You might also need your secretary's home number in case she has to cancel a few meetings.)

- A small flask containing something to fortify you, and to disguise the disinfectant taste of the hospital coffee.

- Toothbrush and toothpaste. One of the most refreshing things you can do after spending hours in a stale room is brush your teeth.

- A pack of cards. If all else fails, a game of solitaire is better than staring at the wall.

Obviously, you'll want to add your own refinements to this basic kit. (A Polaroid camera, for instance, so you can take home pictures to show the new grandparents.) The variations are endless, as long as they all fit into that one small bag.

With luck, you may hit a busy night in the waiting room and find a cast of characters infinitely more entertaining than anything you've brought along. There are several recognizable types of pregnant father. Score 10 points for every one you identify, and give yourself a bonus if you catch them all in the room at the same time.

A guide to who's who in the waiting room

The numbers man
Never goes anywhere without at least four members of his family to give him moral support.

He, his sister-in-law, his brother and two cousins form the basic party, with frequent visits from other relations during the waiting hours. Endless supplies of beer are produced from some mysterious portable store. There is much nervous laughter. As the night wears on, the party breaks up and the numbers man is left alone. He invariably falls asleep in a nest of beer cans just in time to miss the birth of his child.

The office freak
Arrives at the hospital dressed as if to attend a board meeting.

Distinguishing marks: waistcoat, bulging brief-case and a pocket calculator, which he operates with the precision of a concert pianist. From time to time, he consults his watch, but he is confident the baby will arrive well before the stock market opens. Sure enough, it does.

The jitter bug

The classic anxious father. Unable to relax, he prowls around the waiting room and the corridors with rumpled hair and staring eyes. Frequently mistaken for a patient, due to the pyjamas he is wearing under his raincoat. In between circuits of the waiting room, he perches on the edge of a chair, only to spring up in twitching expectation every time the door opens. Such is the unfairness of life that he usually has to wait longer than anyone else, or maybe it just seems that way.

The pro

Watch this one closely if you want to pick up a few pointers on waiting technique. He's been through it all before, and paces himself beautifully. A little light reading to start with, then a short nap in order to be rested and fresh for the great moment. Comes superbly equipped to turn his corner of the waiting room into a home from home. Cordless electric shaver and travelling alarm clock are standard. We have even seen one pro set up a small coffee percolator.

THERE'S ONE BORN EVERY 10 SECONDS*

a random selection of information
and advice that doesn't really fit anywhere else in the book.

<u>Some wildly inaccurate ways of predicting your unborn baby's sex</u>

Guessing the sex has been a favourite preoccupation of pregnant couples ever since pregnant couples first began.

In ancient Egypt, if the mother's face had a greenish tinge, she was definitely carrying a boy (as well as a severe case of indigestion, by the sound of it).

In Russia, dreams of parties were sure signs of the baby being a girl.

The Japanese used to believe that you could guarantee the arrival of a boy by thinking hard of manly pursuits – although a discreet veil is drawn over what particular kind of manly pursuit you should think about.

The march of progress into the middle ages led to a more sophisticated form of prediction: if the woman's right breast grew larger than her left breast, you could expect a boy.

Your wife has none of these symptoms? You can always try listening to her heartbeat during the last three months of pregnancy. A fast rate (144 beats per minute or more) is supposed to indicate a girl; a slow rate of 124 or less, and it's a boy.

In fact, it is now quite possible for your baby's sex to be predicted by scientific tests. But they're

According to the official US birthrate figures for 1974.

not as much fun as measuring the right breast.

On meeting your baby for the first time

"*All* babies", Sir Winston Churchill once said, "look like me". How right he was.

Very new babies are often bald, usually wrinkled and frequently purple with bad temper. Meeting one for the first time can be an alarming experience, even when it's yours.

Be reassured. Within a few days, this odd-looking little creature will turn into the most beautiful baby you've ever seen.

How to be financially delighted when it's triplets or quads

What would you do if instead of one extra mouth to feed, there were two? Or three? Or more?

When the patter of little feet suddenly becomes a stampede, it's difficult to avoid a feeling of complete panic. One baby is expensive; several babies all at once can put you deep into hock for years.*

Fortunately, you can insure against being bankrupted by babies, although it's not easy to arrange a really worthwhile jackpot, as we discovered.

Our first approaches were to big, established insurance companies. Of these, we found only one which would insure against multiple birth, and then only providing the policy was taken out in the first three months of pregnancy. There followed a very reasonable set of questions to establish your medical and family histories. Based on the answers, a premium was quoted.

Then we ran into the big snag, which was that the cover was very limited – the maximum sum they would insure for was £750 for twins and £1500 for triplets or quads. Bearing in mind the multiple sets of clothing and equipment needed, how long do you thing that would last?

Not long enough, we felt, so we then went to an independent insurance broker. He suggested that we try Lloyds, who will insure anything from oil tankers to the weather – for a price. Sure enough, they'll insure against multiple birth as well.

However the maximum sum they will insure for in the United Kingdom is still low – £2000 for twins and £4000 for triplets or quads. Premiums vary considerably according to age,

*Statistically, if your wife is under 20, her chances of giving birth to twins are 1 in 167. By 35, the odds shorten to 1 in 74.

health and family histories, but with no record of twins in either of the parents' families, and no fertility drugs having been taken, a premium as low as 3½% is available.

If you're interested in following up this idea for yourselves, bear in mind the need for speed. Even Lloyds won't insure if the pregnancy is too far advanced. In fact, they require the proposal form to be submitted within the first two months of pregnancy.

The fine art of choosing names

European royal families hedge their bets by equipping their offspring with as many as fourteen different given names. This is a little cumbersome for most of us, although it would be great to have a choice of names when you're old enough to know what *you* want to be called.

The most common mistake in choosing a name comes from forgetting the fiendish tortures that kids inflict on other kids because of an unconventional name, an unfortunate set of initials, or a cute nickname that becomes less cute with every passing year. The agonies of embarrassment suffered by clumsily named children are deeply felt, so use a little foresight when you're choosing.

Breast vs. bottle

At the last count, although 51% of mothers in England and Wales began breast feeding their babies only 4% were still doing so six weeks later.

But despite the figures, breast feeding has some tremendous natural advantages. A healthy mother's milk is always sterile, and delivered at the correct temperature. Minimum preparation is required. The natural formula is superb in terms of nutrition and digestibility. And you, the father, don't have to get up for the 2 a.m. feed.

Right there, we suspect, is the true reason for the overwhelming popularity of the bottle: it means that you can share the feeding chores. On

just about every other count, the bottle comes off second best.

Ah well. Console yourself with the fact that your baby's meal times will conform to more civilized hours after the first three or four months.

How to live at peace with the grandparents

Adopt the same principle that TV networks use with political parties: equal time for both sides.

Unique birth announcement cards

Take a photograph of your baby the first day you go visiting the hospital. Have an express printing service run off as many copies of the photograph as you need. Within three days, you can be mailing a totally original and personal record of your baby's arrival.

Otherwise, make friends with our illustrator, Arthur Robins. He does terrific birth announcement cards, like the one shown here.

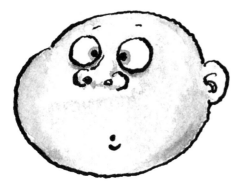

Why new babies are often cross-eyed

Many a new parent has been startled to see the baby's big blue eyes focussed firmly on the end of its nose. Don't panic. The muscles controlling the eyes are not fully developed at birth; hence the erratic behaviour of eyeballs. Within a few days, coordination of muscles and nerves will straighten them out.

How to get a birthday present from the Government

Arrange with your wife that she will give birth before 11.59 p.m. on April 4. If she does, you qualify for a full year's reduction in tax.

Even if nature conspires against you and you miss out on that deadline, there are some other financial consolations.

You will automatically receive a maternity grant of £25, and if your wife has been working she will be eligible for a maternity allowance of £14.70 per week for 18 weeks (these figures are correct for 1977 – they are of course constantly under review).

Other benefits such as free milk and vitamins, free dental treatment and free prescriptions are available, so make sure that you find out what you are entitled to.

The Government has a remarkably soft spot for babies, and you might as well make the most of it.

The world's most fascinating baby toys

For variety, educational value and virtual indestructibility, no toy ever invented can beat parents.

The ideal time to have your second baby

Between two and three years after the birth of your first one.

The age difference is small enough for them to grow up together as close companions. You can get double use from clothes and equipment which would be lost or thrown away if the gap were bigger. And you'll both still be close enough to the memory of nappies and midnight feedings so that a second dose won't be too much of a shock to the system.

How to help your wife get her figure back

You have one final task before you can consider your pregnancy officially over: to act as encourager and chief assistant in the regaining of your wife's pre-baby shape.

Even though it's something you both want, it's not as easy to achieve as you may think. For the first few weeks after the birth, your wife will probably go through an advanced case of anti-climax. The excitement is over, the baby's demands are insistent and tiring, she feels physically and emotionally droopy. Will-power is at a low ebb, and self-indulgence is easier than self-discipline.

Your encouragement is critical in these three main areas.

1. Exercise

Any good baby book (or your doctor) will provide a programme of post-natal exercises to tighten up the muscles that have been stretched during pregnancy and birth. They're very simple, and they don't take up much time – ten minutes a day is about average. But like any exercises, they won't be much use unless they're done regularly, and therein lies the problem. Exercising alone is a gloomy business.

We're not suggesting that you go through the exercises as well (although it certainly wouldn't hurt); but you can at least help by being there to take your wife through the programme. The only way exercise works for most of us is to make it a habit, so put aside a special time each day and *stick to it*. Within three or four weeks, you'll see results.

2. Diet

If you've been sharing your wife's diet during the past nine months, keep it up. Another few weeks isn't going to kill you. If you haven't made any gastronomic concessions so far, now's the time to make them. It may actually be easier now for both of you, since you should see your wife's weight go down, whereas the pregnant diet is at best a holding operation.

You may find it helps to have a weekly weigh-in, or to have a bet on how long it takes your wife to get back to her old fighting weight. The main thing is for you to take an interest in seeing how fast the pounds come off. Dieters love an audience.

3. Incentive

The basic incentive of wanting to be attractive is built in to every woman, and it's a powerful ally in the battle of the bulges. As with dieting, however, it needs a more demonstrative reward than a mirror and a set of bathroom scales.

Let no improvement pass unnoticed, whether it be the loss of a couple of pounds, or half an inch or a new hairstyle. If her waist feels smaller and her stomach firmer, tell her. Even exaggerate a little. Reality will catch up with wishful thinking given enough encouragement.

As more tangible incentives, treat your wife to a new outfit when she gets back down to her old size. Then leave the baby with the grandparents, and go off together for a dirty weekend in a good hotel. Break the diet, pop the cork, and celebrate. You've both earned it.

THE PREGNANT FATHER'S COOKBOOK

with recipes and hints devised, described and illustrated by Len Deighton.

In any pregnancy, no matter how smooth, there are times when a woman's place is anywhere but in the kitchen. She may feel sick, she may feel tired, or she may feel uncomfortable with the growing bulge coming between her and the stove. Whatever the reason, she will be unable to face the thought of cooking.

When this happens to your wife, you have two alternatives: survive on packaged meals, which are expensive and usually revolting; or learn to prepare a few simple but tasty things yourself.

Having tried both ways, we can vouch for the do-it-yourself route. It's more fun and less likely to give you indigestion.

So we asked Len Deighton to give us a few tips which will enable any amateur cook to turn out something that tastes professional. (Before writing spy stories, Mr. Deighton had a weekly cooking column in the *Observer*. He cooks as well as he writes. Maybe better.)

Here he is:

"These recipes are carefully worked out to be simple, provide confidence and produce the sort of food that a wife in bed might like, as well as a harassed husband.

Mostly the recipes are reasonably cheap but quite sophisticated, and flexible enough to give several hundred variations. That's why I included the omelette in spite of the fact that a really good pan is necessary. If our reader doesn't have one I urge him to buy one – then the door opens to every variety of omelette from jam to caviar. The only other things he needs are one wooden spoon and a really heavy pot for stewing. If these are not in the kitchen already then his wife deserves them as presents anyway.

I've kept away from measuring devices except for a wineglass or a 'spoonful'. In any case, the recipes I've chosen don't depend on critically accurate measurements.

It's worth adding that the husband should decide what he's going to cook before he goes out in the morning so that he can do the shopping on the way home. Trying to make meals out of random leftovers is impossible.

I've left out herbs and spices because they introduce too much complexity and their absence in the kitchen might well prove off-putting to the novice cook. All the recipes assume that there's salt and pepper on the table or the tray so they can be added when you eat."

Soups & Sandwiches

How to win at soups - cheat!

Tuna Fish Soup

Mix a can of sweet corn (cream style is best for this) with a can of tuna fish and warm it gently. You'll have to dilute it with milk but don't swamp it. A large spoonful of cream on each bowlful of soup smoothes it and you can sprinkle a tiny pinch of paprika on to the top too, but it doesn't need either.

Pea Soup

A can of peas mashed up with an equal quantity of milk (and some cream too) is much better than any canned pea soup. Serve toast with it.

Tomato Soup

What is true of canned peas is even more true of canned tomatoes. However you'll have to chop up the tomatoes first. Dilute it with consommé rather than milk. This also looks tempting if a thread of cream is flicked over it before it's put on the table.

Consommé

Canned consommé is considerably improved with a teaspoonful of sherry or madeira added to each portion. This is best served with toast too.

Lobster Soup, Chicken Soup, Vichysoisse

All of these need a couple of spoonfuls of cream to brighten them up.

A packet of savoury biscuits – Ritz for instance - can make any soup more attractive. A more ambitious garnish - croutons - can be prepared in five minutes while the soup is heating. Take a slice of white bread, remove the crusts and cut the rest of it into pieces about the size of sugar cubes. Fry these golden in a large spoonful of fat. Butter gives the best colour but burns easily (so keep the heat moderate). Half oil and half butter is easiest to manage but keep stirring and don't leave it unattended. Ideally the croutons are put on to the top of the soup a moment or two before serving.

Sandwiches

Men have a natural aptitude for making sandwiches. Remember to have fresh bread, or rolls, and seek varieties such as pumpernickel, caraway rye, whole wheat, black, French bread or even raisin bread.

Bacon, Lettuce and Tomato - the greatest sandwich of all!

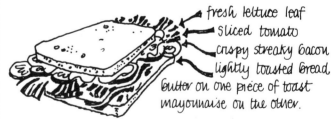

fresh lettuce leaf
sliced tomato
crispy streaky bacon
lightly toasted bread
butter on one piece of toast
mayonnaise on the other.

Sandwich fillings are best bought for the sandwiches rather than using leftovers. What about: liver sausage, hot fried bacon, mashed tinned crab, smoked salmon, hot frankfurters, etc. Hero sandwiches are lengths of French bread split in half lengthwise. Warm toast keeps a hot filling warm longer, so do hot plates. Don't forget the mustard or pickles etc.

2 hrs.
Baked Potato

Do this when you have the oven going for some other dish.

Buy one large potato for each person. Choose ones that are clean and have no eyes, spots or damage.

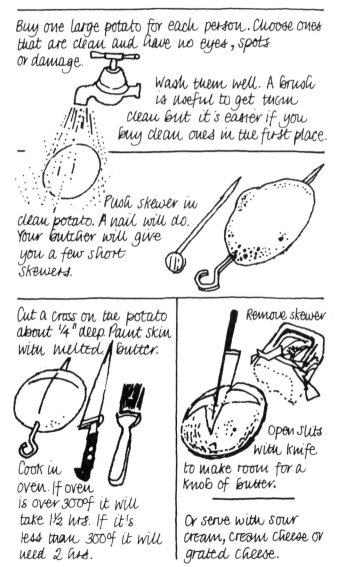

Wash them well. A brush is useful to get them clean but it's easier if you buy clean ones in the first place.

Push skewer in clean potato. A nail will do. Your butcher will give you a few short skewers.

Cut a cross on the potato about ¼" deep. Paint skin with melted butter.

Cook in oven. If oven is over 300°F it will take 1½ hrs. If it's less than 300°F it will need 2 hrs.

Remove skewer

Open slits with knife to make room for a knob of butter.

Or serve with sour cream, cream cheese or grated cheese.

15 mins.
Cabbage

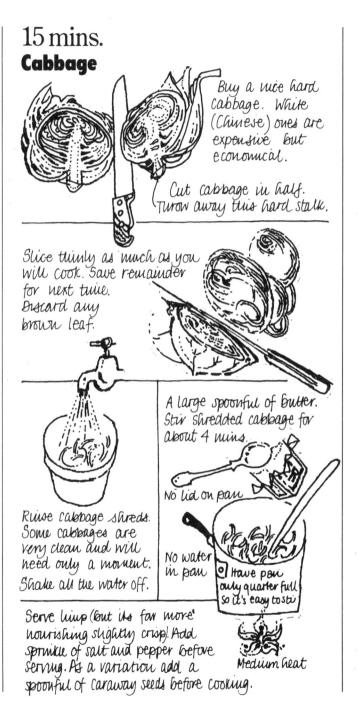

Buy a nice hard cabbage. White (Chinese) ones are expensive but economical.

Cut cabbage in half. Throw away this hard stalk.

Slice thinly as much as you will cook. Save remainder for next time. Discard any brown leaf.

Rinse cabbage shreds. Some cabbages are very clean and will need only a moment. Shake all the water off.

A large spoonful of butter. Stir shredded cabbage for about 4 mins.

No lid on pan

No water in pan

Have pan only quarter full so it's easy to stir

Medium heat

Serve limp (but it's far more nourishing slightly crisp). Add sprinkle of salt and pepper before serving. As a variation add a spoonful of caraway seeds before cooking.

15 mins.
Omelette

A spoonful of filling. Try chopped ham, canned sweetcorn, chopped cheese, jam etc. etc...

An omelette pan is heavy, has no corners and looks like this — you must have one to make omelettes.

A wooden spoon is also useful.

Mix two eggs + ½ shellful of water for each one-person omelette.
Mix so yolks and whites combine.
No need to beat.

Add a little salt and pepper. And mix.

Warm pan on stove for one minute.

From now on to sitting down to eat is only 2 or 3 minutes — so be ready.
High heat.

Pour 3 large spoonsful of cooking oil (any sort) into pan. Wait about ½ minute for oil to heat.

Pour egg into pan.

Use a wooden spoon to drag cooked egg to centre of pan. Tip pan so uncooked egg runs to edge.
(Try to avoid scraping spoon on bottom of pan).

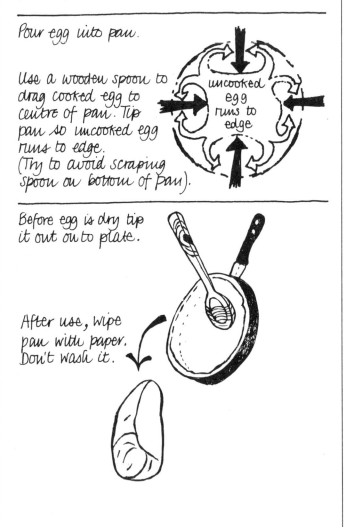

uncooked egg runs to edge

Before egg is dry tip it out on to plate.

After use, wipe pan with paper. Don't wash it.

15 mins.
Salad

Don't do all the variations at once - ring the changes.

Lettuce. Buy clean crisp ones. Pull leaves apart and rinse earth or dirt off. Leave the leaves to drain.

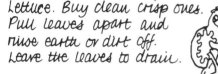

Mix dressing. The better quality the oil and vinegar the better is the salad.

Any spoons

Three parts oil →

One part vinegar →

When you want to eat the salad, put the drained lettuce pieces into any large bowl. Add the oil and vinegar mixture and turn the whole lot over and over until all the leaves are shiny with dressing. SERVE IT.
That is a perfect green salad vinaigrette.

For a more complicated salad add things you like e.g. (make sure they are all clean)

Radishes (whole or sliced)

Raw mushroom (sliced)

Chicory (French : endive) Slice it up.

Tomato slices (not too many, because they are very watery)

Raw cauliflower (small pieces)

Celery - a few pieces

Olives (remove stones even if it means chopping the rest of them very small)

To the dressing you can add
1. A spoonful of bottled mayonnaise
2. A spoonful of blue cheese (break it up with the fork)
3. Garlic. Just rub the bowl with a tiny piece.
4. Anchovy. (tinned ones - take it easy they're salty)

50 mins.
Rice

As a vegetable or as a main meal.

Do it this way, or if you're really in a rush use Instant rice following the instructions on the packet.

Boiling water.

One quick stir.

boiling water about 1/4" higher than rice.
level of rice.

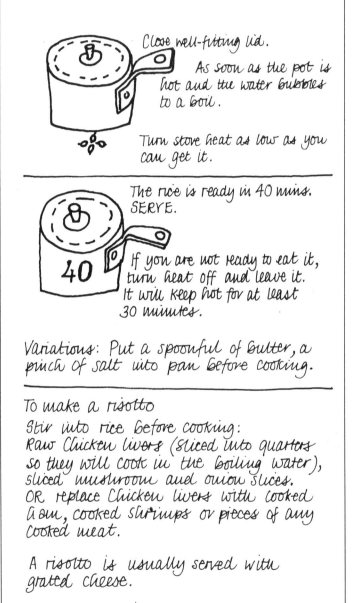

Close well-fitting lid.

As soon as the pot is hot and the water bubbles to a boil.

Turn stove heat as low as you can get it.

The rice is ready in 40 mins. SERVE.

If you are not ready to eat it, turn heat off and leave it. It will keep hot for at least 30 minutes.

Variations: Put a spoonful of butter, a pinch of salt into pan before cooking.

To make a risotto
Stir into rice before cooking:
Raw chicken livers (sliced into quarters so they will cook in the boiling water), sliced mushroom and onion slices.
OR replace chicken livers with cooked ham, cooked shrimps or pieces of any cooked meat.

A risotto is usually served with grated cheese.

1½ hrs.
Roast chicken

Buy a roasting chicken. If it has been frozen it must completely thaw (leave in a cool place for 36-48 hrs.)

Look inside chicken for frozen giblets in plastic bag. Remove them as soon as possible for it prevents the chicken thawing. Better still: buy a fresh chicken _not_ a frozen one (but still make sure there's no plastic bag of giblets inside).

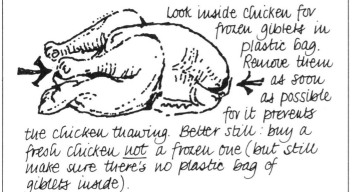

Put chicken into any tin or fire proof dish breast down because the breastmeat goes dry if too cooked.

OR

Put chicken on oven shelf (also breast side down). And put a clean tin on oven floor to catch gravy. This will give you better gravy.

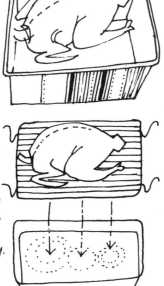

Either way only put chicken in oven when its heated to 350°f.

It will be cooked in 1¼ hours.

Stir a couple of large spoonsful of cream into the gravy and serve it with the chicken.

To cut up the chicken.

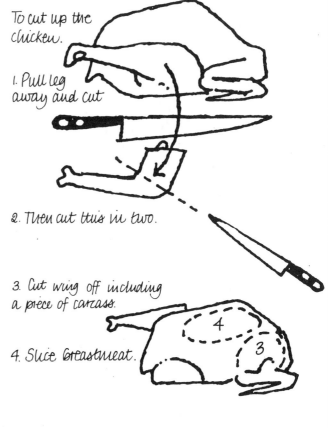

1. Pull leg away and cut

2. Then cut this in two.

3. Cut wing off including a piece of carcass.

4. Slice breastmeat.

4 hrs.
Beef stew

The cheapest possible cut of beef makes the supreme stew. Don't try to improve it by using more expensive cut or removing grey gristle.

This gravy is superb protein for infants from about 4 months old.

Cut 2 lb of Leg of Beef into pieces. Discard white gristle but leave grey gristle. Butcher will have removed bone already.
(The really lazy can cook it all and leave the hard white bits on their plates).
The butcher might chop it for you but be sure you buy Leg of Beef rather than any other cut of meat.

Buy sharp knife

1"

Stage 2.

It's better to have a lid without vent holes.

I like a black iron pot best. A good one will last forever.

Put meat into heaviest pan you can find, with heavy close-fitting lid. Add teaspoon of salt and a pinch of pepper.

Put into oven at 210°F. Gas ovens as low as possible.
Cook 4 hours. SERVE.

210°F

This stew needs no water. The meat will produce its own superb beef gravy.

| If you want to make this into a beef curry stir one tablespoonful of curry powder into the raw beef at Stage 2. | If you want Boeuf bourguignon add a wineglassful of wine at Stage 2. |

If you want Chili con carne add a tin of baked beans and add a dash of tabasco sauce before serving.

Tabasco

40 mins.
Baked fish

This recipe suits many different fish but NOT Herring or Mackerel.

Salmon is fine and expensive. Snapper is the cheapest suitable fish. Sole, Trout or ask your fish merchant for similar ones.

Buy a fish weighing about 1 lb for each person. The dealer will remove the head and clean it.

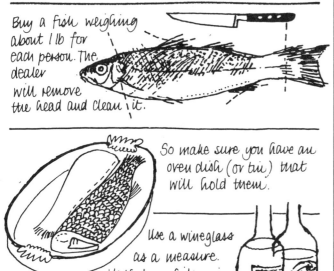

So make sure you have an oven dish (or tin) that will hold them.

Use a wineglass as a measure. Half dry white wine. Half olive oil. Pour this on to fish and turn them over so they are coated with it.

Cook in oven (no lid on dish) for 30 mins at 300°f. Serve on to warm plates.

This is a superb recipe and needs no improvement. However it can be garnished with a thin slice of lemon and some finely chopped parsley.

Fruit bowl

It looks attractive and is very economical because you use only what is eaten.

Buy one or two of each: Tangerines, Dessert Apples, Oranges, Grapefruits, Bananas, Pears and Grapes. Buy again those that get eaten. It's also healthy.

Cheese

Brie: Buy a small wedge. Eat it soon, it's no use for cooking.

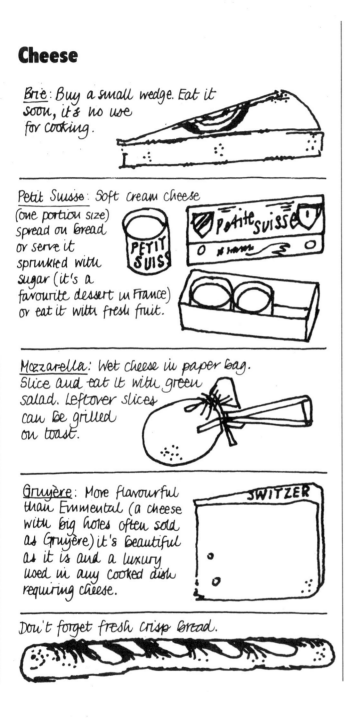

Petit Suisse: Soft cream cheese (one portion size) spread on bread or serve it sprinkled with sugar (it's a favourite dessert in France) or eat it with fresh fruit.

Mozzarella: Wet cheese in paper bag. Slice and eat it with green salad. Leftover slices can be grilled on toast.

Gruyère: More flavourful than Emmental (a cheese with big holes often sold as Gruyère) it's beautiful as it is and a luxury used in any cooked dish requiring cheese.

Don't forget fresh crisp bread.

Bon Appetit!